# THE 7 P

## A LASTING

## MARRIAGE

Rich Nicastro, Ph.D.

Dr. Rich Nicastro

# CONTENTS

# 1. INTRODUCTION

There's a myth floating around in the ether that the most important, complex things in life, the things that verge on the abstract more than the concrete (marriage, for instance, versus, say, getting a driver's license) either work or they don't. And the corollary to that belief is that no amount of plan-fulness can get this complicated facet of your life to work (marriage, for instance) if it's not already going to. The myth goes on to purport that it's better to just "face facts"—after all, the "logic" that stems from illogic tells you, why apply thought or effort or energy to something that's already doomed?

Maybe you've heard the myth. Maybe you've

felt it, sensed it, absorbed it by social osmosis. Maybe you've even believed it at one time or another.

And maybe you're ready to de-*myth*-ify it .

I'm here to tell you that it is, indeed, a myth and not a fact. Over the course of more than twenty years as a psychologist and couples counselor, I've worked with hundreds of couples and have witnessed a high percentage of them turn a less-than-satisfying marriage into a fulfilling marriage.

I've seen couples caught in the cycle of conflict that were sure of only two things when it came to what they brought to the relationship table: (1) they loved each other and (2) in their hearts, they wanted the marriage to work. They knew that love and commitment alone weren't enough to fix their day-to-day problems, but they didn't know what else they needed. Some had partly bought into the myth (I say *partly* because, after all, they were in my office and therefore actively seeking a way to make a difference); some feared there was "nothing we can do" but were still hoping to be proven wrong on that score.

The marriages that last may be incredibly different in many ways (living arrangements, patterns of lovemaking, division of household chores, and the like), but the human pillars within them (the individuals that make up the couple) share certain core characteristics that contribute to their success. And, despite the pesky myth that says those golden-hued elements are either magically bestowed to you or they're forever absent, they are things that can be *learned*.

If our modern society is one that overall values and encourages self-improvement, why are so many of us resigning ourselves to a "that's just the way I am" mindset? Sure, there are some things we can't change about ourselves (if you were hoping to be 6'6" and are a foot shy of that, there's no self-help strategy that can close the gap...that's where loving self-acceptance comes in). But there are just as many things that you *can* change. It comes back, again and again, to whether or not the willingness is there.

Everything that is good and true and meaningful in life begins with a *decision.* Your relationship is no exception.

Before we get to the pillars of a lasting marriage (in this case, the aforementioned traits, not the individuals, the living pillars), I want to distinguish them from the working parts of the relationship. And I'd like to add what feels like another necessary point, too:

Making meaningful, lasting changes to your relationship so that it becomes a meaningful, lasting marriage presupposes two things:

1) You and your partner love each other;

and

2) You and your partner are committed to the relationship.

If you've spent any time on the Internet, you've probably heard self-proclaimed relationship "experts" boast that if you buy their product they promise to save your marriage, no matter what, *even if your partner no longer loves you*, or even if your spouse has moved halfway across the country and started a new life. There's something appealing about that, isn't there? (Something sexy and flashy, even, as so much of today's catchy consumerism is.) It's exhilarating to think that in a relational system that equally involves two people, one person can hold so much sway that s/he can unilaterally pull a marriage from the brink of disaster when the other person has already signed a lease on a new apartment and is even dating someone new.

Because I am a psychologist and therefore operate under a strict—and necessary—code of ethics, I am not going to peddle you a lie. Indeed, there is much one person can do to improve the relationship, without the other partner even knowing that you've cracked a book or taken a seminar. But that presupposes that the other partner isn't already mentally or physically out of the marriage.

So with that important caveat in place, let's look at the components of a marriage/relationship (and please note that I will be using the terms interchangeably...this book is for people considering entering or already in a long-term, committed relationship; whether or not you are married is not the relevant thing here—the level of emotional commitment you have toward your partner and the union is).

Beyond the love and commitment we've already discussed, the other major components of a marriage include communication, intimacy (emotional and sexual), and cooperation. Those are the "working parts" of the marriage, if you will. They are aspects of your relationship that require the two of you to engage in (you can't communicate, cooperate, or have sex alone). But what feeds these mutually-experienced components? What keeps communication and sexual intimacy and cooperation working? (And not just working, but enriching and enhancing your bond.) What holds them up?

The pillars.

The 7 pillars of a lasting marriage are habits you can decide to take up on your own, right now, whether your mate is on board or not. And the positive changes you make will positively impact the working parts of your relationship...those changes may also positively impact your partner's behavior. I've witnessed that in couples where one individual stops blaming and decides to "be the change s/he wants to see in the relationship" (to slightly tweak Gandhi's sage advice) and the other partner gradually, positively shifts as well. (You've probably witnessed how moods are contagious, whether they're bad moods or good moods. This is the kind of thing that can happen in marriages, where the new, healthy relationship patterns implemented by one partner "infect" the other partner and strengthen the marriage overall.)

I'll briefly introduce the pillars of a lasting marriage now, and then will discuss each of them in more detail in the coming chapters. We'll look at examples of couples that illustrate the pillars in a "live" way. Each section also includes questions to take you further, self-reflective queries that, if you approach them with good intentions and responsibility for your own thoughts and actions (rather than with the agenda to change your partner's), will start to shift your mindset to a pro-relationship one, even if you believe you don't currently exemplify the pillar-traits.

## The Seven Pillars of a Lasting Marriage:

### Empathy

Can you put yourself in your partner's shoes? Can you imagine what it feels like to be him/her? Can you see him/her as an ally— and more like you than unlike you—even in the midst of an argument? This will naturally help you be a more loving and responsive partner and also will shift your perspective in what can be remarkable ways.

## Mindfulness

What does it mean to be a mindful spouse? Couples have a great deal of power and influence over each other, and too often this fact is ignored or forgotten. Our primary means of influence are the words we use to express ourselves to our partner. You can make the decision to make your partner feel loved, supported, and connected through what you say to him/her. And making that particular decision doesn't take any more time or effort than making the decision to choose words (or gestures) that push your partner away (or worse, belittle or demean him/her).

## Humility

Sometimes people think expressing humility

means giving away your power. Not at all.
True humility doesn't mean becoming a
doormat; it means putting aside arrogance
and the belief that your way is always the
best way.

## Openness/Presence

Openness and presence in your marriage
require you to remove the clutter from your
mind so that you can be more fully engaged
with your partner in the moment. It's hard
to put into words exactly what it is, but
presence is something your partner will *feel*
(and s/he will certainly feel the *lack* of
your presence, even though you may be
sitting an inch away). Some things that
oppose presence are: distraction, being too
quick to reply to something your partner has
said, or reacting emotionally to your
partner's message or in some way that pulls
you out of the moment.

When you are not laboring under an
arrogant mindset that sends your partner the
message (unspoken or otherwise) that his/her

reaction to something is unwarranted or over the top, you can be genuinely open to what your partner is needing from you, as well as open to the gifts that s/he brings to the relationship.

## Enthusiasm/Curiosity

Not everyone can be enthusiastic all the time, and certainly we all show it in different ways. My wife, for instance, is a self-described "gusher," while I am much more quiet and even-keeled in my responses. Someone who didn't know me might think I wasn't enthusiastic at all if they witnessed my wife and I both reacting to the same piece of good news.

However, my wife can tell when I'm enthusiastically listening to something she's communicating, or when I'm enthusiastically sharing something I'd like her to be actively present for. True enthusiasm can't be faked (at least not with the ones who know us best). And true enthusiasm occurs alongside *curiosity*: you can't get excited about something going on for your partner if you're typically not curious about your mate overall.

As with each of these seven pillars, the goal isn't to force yourself into feeling something you're not—it's to *foster* healthy, pro-relationship mindsets that are already within you, but that you may have neglected for a while.

## Gratitude

Do you feel grateful for what you already have in your life, or are you only focused on what's lacking? While part of self-improvement is identifying areas where change is desired, if you stop there and fail to foster an "attitude of gratitude," any changes you make will likely be short-lived or will not bring you long-term satisfaction.

## Honesty

Are you expressing an honest message? This

doesn't mean you have to be cruel ("Wow, honey, that dress makes you look a sofa!"). Rather, are you contributing honesty to the relationship, or are you adding deception into the mix? Are you being your authentic self or are you closing your true self off? You'd be amazed at how many people are less than honest with their mates on a regular basis and then are indignant when they discover they've been lied to. What you put into the relationship tends to come back to you.

So there you have it, a brief overview of the 7 pillars of a lasting marriage.

I'm often asked about my own marriage. And the spirit of the questioning is something like, "With all your training and experience and knowledge, your marriage must be problem-free." Not at all. Like you, I have to make conscious decisions about which elements I will bring to my marriage. For instance, will I choose humility, even when I am doggedly *sure* I'm "right," or will I choose the arrogance that steamrolls my wife's point of view? (And if I choose the latter, this means I won't even be *hearing* her point of view.)

Sometimes I'll hear myself giving relationship advice to a couple and wonder why I didn't try that in my own marriage. So *knowing* the right thing to do doesn't guarantee *doing* the right thing. Just like you, I see my marriage as a work-in-progress. Like yours, my marriage is rewarding, meaningful, evolving, challenging, but worth the challenges. There is no such thing as perfection, not in individuals or couples, so that's not what I'm striving for. Rather, I strive to be a husband that I hope my wife feels glad to be married to. And I do this through daily decisions—the small stuff—and when I forget and make a mistake, I accept responsibility (meaning, I don't point a finger at my wife) and try again. Yes, *knowing* what's beneficial to relationships is critical (and that's where this and other books come in), but it's only the first step. The *doing* is what is ongoing and decision-driven and in each and every one of our hands.

For those of you curious about where the pillars came from, they took shape for me gradually, over many years of working with couples in counseling and many years giving workshops for couples. I started to notice similarities between successful couples, and, over time, I began to distill those commonalities into characteristics that supported relationships. Many of these couples would probably be surprised at the thought that they were exemplifying these traits; most likely, they weren't exhibiting the pillars in a self-conscious way and labeling what they were doing. But I took note.

It's sort of like how we can all speak just fine, but probably a very small percentage of us would be able to diagram a sentence and label the parts of speech. (I doubt I'd be able to!) You're effectively using speech; you don't need to label the parts...the usage is what matters. Similarly, the couples already incorporating these pillars into their marriage are benefitting from the enhanced support they give; whether they can name the pillars isn't the point.

Before I close this introduction, I'd like to take a moment to thank the people who specifically requested this book. I've also written two other books (*Communication Breakthrough* and *Hurt By the One You Love: The Power of Forgiveness in Intimate Relationships*), but those are longer than this one and deal with more specific topics. Some of my clients and readers of my blog asked for something they could read in one or two sittings and something that could help them contribute to the health of their relationship overall, rather than pinpointing communication and forgiveness as the other books do.

I hope you enjoy reading the book as much as I enjoyed planning it and writing it, and I hope the pillars fortify your marriage in a way that brings you and your partner closer than ever.

# 2. EMPATHY

"The love of our neighbor in all its fullness simply means being able to say to him, 'What are you going through?'" ~Simone Weil

## Meet Russell and Lana

Married for three years, Russell and Lana described their marriage as "solid overall." However, they'd been struggling with one issue in particular for awhile. You've probably heard that the most frequently fought-about topics for couples are sex and money. Russell and Lana's fights fell into the latter category.

"We have good jobs," Russell said to me at their first couples counseling session. "So I don't get why Lana gets so upset when I buy something big-ish or when I suggest a major trip."

"C'mon, Russ, don't make it sound innocuous. Why don't you tell Dr. Nicastro about the ATV you bought without telling me, and how you were insulted when I didn't do cartwheels over the 'surprise.'"

"Hey, that was for both of us!" Russell said. "Not just for me."

Lana sighed. "The point was that it was a major purchase, and you're not supposed to be making those without checking with your wife."

"And if I had checked?" Russell said.

"Would you have said yes?"

Lana didn't answer, which encouraged Russell to say, "Exactly! Look, I swear I don't do this to make you uncomfortable, but babe, we've got the money for what we want. I just don't see a reason to hoard it."

Lana turned to me. "Doctor, when we have this discussion at home, at this point he calls me controlling. Accuses me of having an agenda, says I want to take away his freedom and that I don't want him to enjoy life." She paused. "That's *so* not what I'm about."

Before I could respond, Russell jumped in and said, "What else could it be?"

I turned to Russell and asked, "It seems like this complaint is only about money and doesn't play out in any other aspect of your relationship. Is that correct?"

He said it was.

"So," I continued, "is it fair to say that you don't feel controlled by Lana in any other circumstance?"

"That's true," Russell conceded.

I encouraged the couple to continue to talk about this issue to see if something fruitful would come of their discussion in the office, but they became more and more defensive until it was clear that the listening process (and therefore the communication process in general) had shut down completely.

"And this is how it usually goes," Lana concluded. "He calls me stingy, and I call him a spendthrift, and nothing ever gets resolved."

What stood out for me in witnessing their exchange—but what wasn't getting picked up on by Russell—was that Lana felt *anxious* about money. And as long as this underlying anxiety wasn't explored, I predicted that Russell would continue to interpret what she was saying as an effort to control him.

Empathy requires us to hear our partner at different levels. Not just the words themselves, but the undercurrent of feeling that carries the words. So, in other words, true empathy asks you to consider where your partner's beliefs or reactions may be coming from, rather than only considering how those beliefs and reactions appear on the surface and how they impact you.

At a very deep level, empathy is a special kind of listening. It's about hearing your partner in ways that no one else might. So a lack of empathy, ultimately, is a type of breakdown in communication and connection—it's a failure to hear your partner deeply and fully, and therefore a failure to *join* your partner wherever they are in the moment.

At this point, I turned to Lana and asked, "What is it that you would like Russell to hear that he's not hearing? What is he missing that's frustrating you?"

"I don't like when he calls me controlling. It makes me feel unheard and unseen."

"Sorry," Russell mumbled.

"What is it that you need him to see?" I prompted.

"I know we're okay financially right now. I get that. But what happens if the bottom drops out? What happens if we lose our jobs?"

"Honey," Russell rushed in. "I've told you, that's not going to happen. But if it does, we'll get new jobs."

"You don't know that, Russ. It's a scary world out there." She turned to me. "Dr. Nicastro, after my dad got sick, we had nothing growing up. My brother and I had to live with relatives who weren't all that happy to have us because my mother couldn't afford to feed us. It was awful."

Russell put an arm around her shoulder and pulled her closer. She seemed grateful for the touch.

"My parents were doing okay before then," Lana said softly. "They didn't expect to become impoverished. Russell says there's no way anything like that could happen to us, but no one knows for sure what the future holds."

Empathic listening in this moment involved

28

Russell tuning in to the fear and insecurity driving Lana's money concerns. When he started to listen at this level, an emotional softening occurred. Rather than see her as controlling, he saw her as someone who was afraid. She feared losing the financial security that had eluded her parents, and that therefore had eluded her in childhood.

Money was an issue that triggered core insecurities in her. While it seemed natural that Russell would define it as a means for her to control him, that was missing the bigger picture of her life. When he could manage to get himself (and his perspective) out of the way as much as possible and imagine what it was like for her growing up as a child, he was practicing empathy and therefore opening up a means for deeper listening and emotional connection.

Although he had known about Lana's childhood for years, he wasn't using that knowledge to put himself in her shoes. (Empathy requires this.) And this shows that we must set the intention and make decisions to practice empathy, because vital information about our partner can easily be forgotten at the cost of meaningful communication.

As Russell's example illustrates, you can know about something and let the knowledge retreat to the back of your mind. Or you can know about something and let the knowledge inform your listening and therefore inform how you react to your partner.

## Can you be a more empathic spouse?

One of the truisms I've learned in my work as a psychologist and couples counselor is that healthy marriages and relationships are *created*, not found. And to create a relationship that brings fulfillment to your life takes a certain set of relationship tools or skills.

While there are many different skills that can help you build a stronger union (e.g., effective communication skills), one of the most important relationship skills is the ability to meaningfully understand your spouse's point of view—to empathize or to see the world through his/her eyes.

Empathy acts as a bridge to your partner's psychological and emotional world, thereby increasing understanding, deepening mutual trust and, ultimately, intimacy (empathic responses can deepen both emotional intimacy and physical intimacy).

But empathy isn't always easy...

Improving a skill takes practice. The belief that mutual understanding should be automatic in loving relationships (and not require ongoing effort) is dangerous and can, over time, erode the foundation of your marriage.

It's important for you to take the time and energy needed to improve your empathic ability in an effort to increase the trust and intimacy that is central to the health of your relationship.

**What's needed for empathy to thrive in your marriage?**

*You must give you partner permission to have her/his own reactions.*

As the differences between you and your partner become apparent over time, so will the frustrations inherent in some of those differences. Very often dissimilarities are viewed as obstacles rather than assets that bring life and energy to a partnership.

Establish a daily intention to challenge yourself any time you think your mate "should" be feeling a certain way—a way that makes sense to you; a way that's similar to how *you* would react. Establishing intentions that acknowledge and appreciate differences can be a powerful means to change.

You may literally need to repeat to yourself: "*She is not me. She's her own person with her own way of seeing the world. She has every right to her reactions.*" After repeating this to yourself several times, repeat it another ten times. As is the norm when learning any new skill, consider repetition the rule of thumb in shifting attitudes that prohibit empathy.

This process can be helpful because it is often our own emotional reactions and viewpoints that block us from empathizing and appreciating our partner's reactions (and unique perspectives). Remember, in doing this, you're not required to abandon your own perspective, but rather, you are temporarily placing your perspective on hold so that you can be a more understanding and empathic spouse.

## Empathy 101:    Flex your imagination muscle

Marital conflict is a given in any long-term union. Couples who resist this reality (by holding the unrealistic expectation that "true love" should result in eternal harmony) will sooner or later find themselves unprepared for the inevitable tides of misunderstandings that will require compromise, some creative problem-solving, and the need for mutual give-and-take.

But just because relationship conflict is to be expected doesn't mean that you and your spouse/partner cannot learn the skills needed to effectively communicate in order to get your needs met, reduce unnecessary arguments, and build better understanding and emotional intimacy.

At times (maybe even often) your spouse's response will differ from your own—e.g., you're able to let something quickly roll off your back while your partner is ruminating for two days about the exact same event.

But this is where many couples get stuck—I see it all the time with the couples who seek my help. When your partner's reaction is very different from your own, the easy way out is to judge him/her for their reactions rather than putting in the time and effort to understand them.

Empathy can build a bridge of understanding and emotional connection between you and your partner.

True empathy involves the ability to *imagine* what it is like for your partner, independent of how you would respond. If your partner is nervous about trying something new (something you don't find intimidating), the goal should be to suspend your immediate reaction and imagine what it must be like for her/him. And it's important to remember that true empathy does not include *judgment*. You can't try to *imagine* what a situation is like for someone else when you're *judging* how they're reacting to the situation. Judgment keeps you stuck in your own perspective and therefore far removed from your partner's.

## Self-Reflective Moment

While you might not understand why this *particular* situation is causing your mate to feel afraid, you do know about the experience of fear (or joy, excitement, anger, sadness, etc.). Practice being empathic by remembering a time when your reaction was similar to your partner's, even though the events that led up to your reaction differ. This can help you break down any resistance that may be blocking you from entering into your spouse's emotional world.

It isn't necessary to share the details of the situation that led to your feelings at that moment; instead, use your emotional reaction (the one that parallels your partner's) to give you a better appreciation of what it is like to be your partner in that moment.

And try to communicate from this place of greater appreciation and empathy.

## Anticipating the need for empathy

I'd like to share a communication strategy that I believe we all should be practicing in our relationships: It's called **anticipatory empathy.** (The concept of anticipatory empathy comes from Relational-Cultural Theory—RCT.) Here is the definition of anticipatory empathy according to RCT:

"Using one's attunement and understanding of an individual to predict the possible impact of one's words or actions on another person; a therapist constantly tries to use anticipatory empathy to get a sense of what might ensue following a particular intervention in therapy."

Practicing anticipatory empathy would force us to hit the pause button on our knee-jerk reactions by taking a self-reflective moment: A brief introspective instant where we bring our spouse into clearer mental focus and imagine how our words and message would possibly impact him/her. Of course, doing so requires ongoing practice and patience. But the communication payoff is huge.

## Self-reflective moment

The goal is to become more responsible and thoughtful communicators, making intentional efforts to choose particular words that more gently convey our truth rather than words that would (intentionally or unintentionally) emotionally wound and feed defensiveness.

So the next time you and your partner are going to have an important discussion, begin to slow down the process and momentarily reflect on which words would best convey your message and which would best honor the love and respect you feel for your mate.

And if you reflect on how you much or how little you've been using empathy in your marriage up to this point, don't get discouraged or beat yourself up if you've used it little or not at all. Most of the time, failing to be empathic is not due to malice or meanness or deliberately withholding something we know our partner needs. There are two basic reasons why we typically don't move toward empathy during times when our spouse needs it:

1) You might be upset with how your partner is handling a situation, and that anger (or other strong emotion) causes you to only see how your spouse "should" be dealing with the circumstance. Because the "should" is a type of judgment, it's the opposite of empathy, and indeed, it blocks the empathic response.

2) You might be overwhelmed with your own feelings (that have nothing to do with your partner's situation). You might be stressed or fatigued or anxious about something, and therefore you're already spread thin, running on fumes emotionally. Therefore, it would feel too overwhelming to put yourself in your partner's shoes. It might feel impossible, like you just don't have the inner resources at hand for that.

So you can see that empathic failings are human and understandable. The good news is that you can make a commitment to try to have the empathic successes outweigh the failings. As with all the pillars we'll discuss, empathy is a trait you can become more mindful of and can practice bringing into your marriage more and more.

## Questions to take you further:

Before we leave the empathy section and explore the next pillar, I'd like to present you with some questions to consider. You might share these with your partner, or you might reflect on them alone. Either way, it's important to note that the effort of nurturing and maintaining a strong relationship first happens at the level of thought. Therefore, having productive questions in your mind is a valuable means of keeping your relationship moving in the right direction.

Since no two relationships are exactly alike, the answers to these questions are uniquely yours, and they may change as time goes on. So feel free to revisit them as your relationship matures and deepens.

1) Are there things that you can identify that stand in the way of you being a more empathic spouse? Are there particular reactions/emotions that you typically have a harder time empathizing with? If so, why do

you think this is? (Focus on you...this is not an exercise in finger-pointing. Remember, you can be a more empathic partner even if your mate stays exactly the same.)

2) Think back to a time when you needed empathy from someone (this doesn't have to be your spouse), and instead, you felt judged or shut-down. Contrast that with a time when someone was empathically supportive of you. Note the differences between those two experiences, especially how you felt when you knew the other person was miles away from your perspective versus when you felt emotionally validated and nurtured by the other. What can you take away from these experiences with the goal of mindfully turning to empathy whenever possible in your marriage?

3) To be on the receiving end of empathy, it's vital that you allow yourself to be known by your partner. If you close your honest-authentic self off to your mate, s/he

can't know what your emotional needs are in the moment. So just as giving empathy requires certain things of you, receiving empathy does as well. At times, it asks you to make yourself vulnerable by sharing your pain with your spouse. There are inherent risks in this (which is why sometimes we shy away from it; we'd rather not court rejection), but there are also great rewards, for you *and* your marriage.

With that said, what steps can you take to clearly express what you're needing from your partner, as well as giving your spouse feedback when s/he is being empathic in a way that works for you, and when s/he misses the mark? This feedback should be given in a kind and loving way; in essence, you are informing your partner about what empathy looks like for you.

# 3. MINDFULNESS

"The highest possible stage in moral culture is when we recognize that we ought to control our thoughts." ~Charles Darwin

**Mindfulness in marriage** starts with you. It starts with the thoughts you think and the words you say to yourself.

The power of words can't be overestimated. Undoubtedly, they impact people. They stir feelings and cause us to react. Sometimes the impact is immediate and dramatic. At other times, the language we use drives our relationships in subtle ways. But the power behind this subtleness shouldn't be minimized. Over time, these quieter moments accumulate, shaping the terrain of our relationship in ways that can nurture openness and intimacy or create powerful communication barriers (which undermine the emotional connection we are seeking).

Becoming aware of how your words are impacting your partner is what mindfulness in marriage is all about. Stay mindful of the influence of your words upon your mate, thereby being a good steward of your language. (It will help to recall the concept of anticipatory empathy that we discussed in the previous chapter.)

In couples counseling, one or both partners may complain about having little or no power to influence the course of their relationship. Such disempowerment distresses us. Just imagine your relationship is slipping through your fingers and there is little-to-nothing you can do to stop this unraveling. Such helplessness can make us feel crazy at times, pushing us to extremes in a desperate attempt to change things (though such extreme reactions usually just make things worse).

But it turns out that these disenfranchised couples actually have significant power, even though they might not define it as such.

Their words shaped by helplessness and defensiveness continue to inadvertently feed the very helplessness they are railing against. Lobbing accusations at your partner in an effort to get him/her to act in more loving ways seldom brings about the desired outcome.

Rather, your accusations (even if partly accurate) can continually incite your partner's defensiveness and widen the emotional divide between you. In these instances, the power of your words inadvertently creates intimacy barriers that lead you to feel helpless, a helplessness that feeds back to and shapes the ways in which you communicate.

## Barriers to connection in marriage start with the words we say to ourselves

When we're having a particular emotional experience, the way we capture the experience and communicate it to ourselves (and then, to others, if we choose) is through words.

*I'm a competent and capable person;*

*I can do whatever I put my mind to;*

*I feel so lost without her. My heart literally hurts;*

*I hate when he talks to me like that. I feel like I'm the child and he's the parent;*

*I'm worried about our financial future if he doesn't take this job;*

*I never get what I want, I'm just an unlucky person.*

The above statements are examples of the words we use to *identify* and *capture* our experience. The process of naming our experiences helps give shape and clarity to what we're feeling; it helps us make sense of the unfolding and ephemeral nature of our inner world. Our words act like a verbal thumb tack, holding our experience in place so we can examine it fully.

Now let's look at that last statement above a little closer:

"I *never* get what I want, I'm just an *unlucky* person."

This *feels* like a *truth* to the person *saying* or thinking it.

I feel this way because it is true and that's why I'm saying it (naming it to myself).

**Feeling + truth = words I choose to describe the experience**

So in this equation, our words are thought to simply reflect a truth within us (there is a **one-way directional** influence here; our inner truth/experience causes us to use certain words).

But what if the *choice* of words also shapes what we're experiencing, by either intensifying the experience, helping to maintain it over time, or biasing it in some way?

In particular, what impact might the choice of the words NEVER and UNLUCKY have on this person's view of him/herself and of his/her future experiences?

## How our words/beliefs act as filters, allowing or excluding certain experiences

Language extremes (words like *always*, *never*) are powerful shapers of experience.

These extremes blot out nuances, diluting the multitude and richness of experiences that we come across on a daily basis.

And these word extremes prevent us from identifying any *exceptions* that may contradict (rather than confirm) their extremeness. For instance, how many times did the person holding the belief "I *never* get what I want" actually get what s/he wanted but this getting-what-I-want experience had no place to land and be recognized? Language extremes (saying, "I *never*..." or "You *always*...") constrict our perceptions, biasing the information that gets psychologically tagged as relevant or irrelevant.

In this equation, there is a **bi-directional influence** between the words we choose to describe our experiences and the actual experiences themselves.

I *feel* this way because it is *true* and that's why I'm *thinking/saying* it. And the words I'm *choosing* to capture my experience are *altering* the very experience they are being used to describe.

**How our words shape our partner's experiences (including her/his experience of us)**

When we mindlessly lob words like "always" and "never" back and forth at each other, it's usually not to highlight each other's virtues ("You *always* treat me with respect. You're the best!"; "You *never* get impatient; I'm so blessed to have you in my life!").

Rather it's usually to point out shortcomings that are driving us a little crazy ("You *always* forget to call or text when you're running late. I've asked you a thousand times to be considerate but you *never* listen to me!"; "You *always* jump out of bed right after we're done having sex! Why can't you just stay with me for a while after we make love?").

Nothing gets us more defensive than being on the receiving end of an *always* or *never* accusation. I've seen such statements enrage people during counseling sessions and I've witnessed how quickly these statements can shut someone down.

⇒ always

⇒ never

⇒ every time

⇒ all the time

⇒ without fail

⇒ constantly

These words/phrases handcuff us emotionally by implying an ongoing and consistent wrongdoing without any exceptions. Our efforts and any forward movement we've made are denied. And in the face of such sweeping accusations, we end up feeling helpless (and shut down emotionally) and/or indignant (and defend ourselves by counter-attacking).

It deserves repeating: Such indictments ignore our efforts to improve the relationship, while also overlooking any *exceptions* that exist in addition to what isn't working (for example, your wife has been more affectionate over the last month, but the recent marriage conflict has erased these improvements from your mind).

## Communicating frustration (rather than truth)

When these indictments come out of our

mouth, they usually reflect our
frustrations.

We're exasperated, we've had this
conversation with our partner a hundred
times before and s/he acts like it never
happened. We may have done our best to
communicate effectively (and sensitively) in
order to get our message across to our
partner. And we may have even been promised
some kind of change...only to have the
promise fall flat. Who wouldn't be pulling
their hair out under these circumstances?

These frustrations should be acknowledged,
because once acknowledged, a more balanced
conversation can occur. "I know you don't do
it all the time, but it's just so
frustrating when it happens again. We've
talked about this..."

Here the goal is to be mindful of our
frustrations and how our frustrations push
us toward extremes in perception (You're
*constantly*... "). The antidote to these
communication barriers is to sensitively
express our frustrations, not to allow our
frustrations to blindly choose our words for

us.

Remember, your relationship frustrations shape your perception and your choice of words (the descriptives used to capture your experience); *and* your choice of words calcifies your experience in ways that can lead to certain biases (thinking your partner always acts a certain way prevents you from seeing the times when s/he acts in ways that dis-confirm or challenge your expectations).

This is why being **mindful** of the language you use to make sense of your own experiences and communicating your experiences to your partner is vital to staying in control of the communication process.

Being on the receiving end of such verbal extremes saps our motivation to continue our efforts to improve our marriage. If my last two screw-ups nullify the three prior successes, then I'm probably going to throw my hands up and think, "Why should I even bother? Nothing I do matters."

Be mindful of the power of your words (even when the frustrations about your partner are making you feel anything but powerful). So take some time to think about the words you typically use to describe what is and isn't working in your marriage or relationship.

And after an honest assessment, try to bring *balance* and *nuance* to the words/phrases you use to describe your feelings (to yourself) as well as the words/phrases you communicate to your spouse.

## Becoming a mindful spouse, one decision at a time

Each day you make decisions that impact your health: Saying "no" to a second piece of cheesecake, deciding on the brown rice rather than white, spending thirty minutes on the exercise bike, meditating for ten minutes...

And the same goes for your relationship—you are continuously making decisions that impact the health of your marriage/relationship (for good or for bad, whether you're consciously aware of each and every decision or not).

## The power of mindful decisions

Every single day you interact with your partner in a multitude of ways and say or do things that can either strengthen or undermine your marriage. Reacting automatically (and unconsciously) is always an option, though, of course, this approach isn't recommended.

The goal is to become more mindful of how you act (and react) with your partner each day—to slow down what feels like automated, beyond-your-control responses ("My wife said something to push my buttons, so of course I got angry!"; "He knows that drives me crazy and he did it anyway, so I had no choice but to blow up!").

An important step in creating (co-creating) a healthy relationship is becoming present and aware of the choices you make from moment-to-moment. In order for this to occur, you must see yourself with new eyes—with an awareness that challenges the belief that even when it feels like your reactions are the result of your spouse's behavior, ultimately you have the power to decide what to say and how to act. In a word, this means choosing mindfulness over the mindless, customary knee-jerk reactions that we so often slip into.

To feel empowered, more fully present and in control of your reactions, it will be important to set an intention to raise your consciousness regarding the decisions you make with your partner (with each interaction you're faced with a **decision-point** — a particular moment where you can recognize the options available to you).

**3 questions to help set daily mindfulness intentions:**

1)    Today, how can I act and react in ways that contribute to a stronger, healthier relationship?

2) How can I consciously avoid acting and reacting in ways that hurt or undermine my marriage today?

3) Will I fall back on the familiar ways of being and act in ways that simply feed the status quo of the relationship? Or will I consciously strive to do better?

Reflecting on these questions before you jump into the routines of your day will help you prime your mind to a new level of awareness and empowerment. Remember, the goal is to make healthy choices for your marriage even when it feels like your partner isn't (I know, easier said than done). Your positive changes in behavior can gradually break any negative cycles of interaction that have taken over your relationship, and they can deepen intimacy in an already strong relationship.

*The choice is yours.*

# Creating a mindful marriage: resist the "automated life" syndrome

Stefan's Story

Stefan isn't enthusiastic about his job; in fact, he does the bare minimum just to get through the day and avoid being fired. While at work he approaches tasks in a mindless way:

• He rarely changes his routines or his approach to the tasks at work:

• His expectations are set in stone. He anticipates that each day will basically be the same as the previous, and this leaves him uninspired; these expectations narrow Stefan's experiences and have a dramatic impact on how he relates to others;

• He gives little (if anything) of himself emotionally or intellectually while at work;

• He's not committed to the success of the company ("I figure I'd find another job if the business goes belly-up").

To make matters worse, Stefan approaches his marriage the same way he does his job, so it's no surprise that there are significant problems and that he's talking about throwing in the relationship towel.

*Mindlessness* takes little effort on your part. You know that mindlessness has set in when life and/or your marriage take on an automated quality (it's as if you're carried through life by the mere repetition of your daily routines).

Many marriages fall prey to mindlessness. What's the alternative?

## The mindful marriage: creating mindful relatedness

One of Stefan's coworkers, Andrea, holds a similar job position as Stefan, yet they are miles apart—Andrea approaches her work and life in a mind*ful*, fully conscious way.

Andrea's Story

• Andrea deliberately changes her routines from time to time, which helps break the monotony of work;

• She isn't a prisoner of rigid expectations that narrow her experiences— she's open to and welcomes novelty, even the smallest changes that could easily go unnoticed if she didn't remain open to them;

• She shows up to work each day ready to engage emotionally and intellectually with whatever the day might bring. This creates emotional richness in her relationships, and when problems arise that need attention, she approaches them with zeal;

• Her approach to work leads to a daily commitment to do her best; her effort is what she finds rewarding, no matter how trivial or tedious the task might seem to others.

Andrea's work-life holds important lessons that can help us all build and maintain a stronger marriage or committed relationship. In fact, her relationship with her husband of seventeen years has greatly benefited from her mindfulness.

## The four principles of mindfulness

1. Increase awareness of your expectations— the expectations that can act as blinders and keep you seeing the "same old things" day in and day out;

2. Show up each day fully present (emotionally, intellectually, spiritually) and ready to engage and share yourself with your partner;

3. Create balance: pepper the familiar and routine with doses of novelty when possible;

4. Celebrate the process (rather than being overly focused on the outcome): In other words, remain aware that your best *effort*

(independent of the results) is what's meaningful; this is an act of commitment to your marriage.

Utilizing these four mindfulness principles takes self-discipline, but the results to your relationship are well worth your effort. So as you revisit the above four points, think about how you can begin applying mindfulness to your marriage...today.

**Mindful marriage self-reflection action step:**

Here's a suggestion to help get you started: Each morning, ask yourself, "How can I show up today in my marriage as if I'm showing up for the first day of a new job?"

If you give this question serious attention, I think you'll be surprised by what you come up with!

I hope this message allows you to see your relationship (or some aspect of your relationship) in a new light.

## Questions to take you further:

1)  Mindfulness begins by setting the
intention to increase awareness of the
impact your decisions and words have on your
partner. What steps can you take to set the
daily mindfulness intention of becoming more
aware about the ways in which your words and
actions affect your spouse?


2)  Knowing your partner's sensitivities and
emotional triggers, what words/statements
should you avoid using with your partner? If
your spouse were asked the same question
about *your* sensitivities and emotional
triggers, how do you think s/he would
respond?

  What alternatives can you use that honor
what you are trying to communicate while
taking into account his/her particular
sensitivities? (And try to answer this
question from your mate's point of view,
too, regarding alternative statements for
your emotional triggers.)

3) What does it mean to you to live mindfully? Do you ever feel like you're going through the motions at work or at home and that you're not fully present, even to yourself? (We've all had the experience of driving a familiar route and realizing that once we got to our destination, we had almost no memory of the actual drive there.)

How can you slow down each day to break this dream-like stupor and attend to the present moment in a way that allows you to be more fully engaged with your mind and with whatever task is at hand?

# 4. HUMILITY

"Humility is not thinking less of yourself, it's thinking of yourself less." ~C.S. Lewis

**What is humility? And what does it mean to be humble?**

Humility is a stance toward oneself; it's how you position yourself in the world and in relation to others. To have humility or to be humble means you do not elevate yourself in importance in relationship to those in your life.

Love doesn't automatically promote humility. In order to make humility a regular part of your marriage, you must set the intention to be humble. You'll need to

attempt to see your experiences and your
partner's experience through the lens of
humility.

Why is this essential to your relationship?

**Let's look at what a humility mindset can
bring to your marriage:**

1. Humility lays the groundwork for the
dynamic of mutuality. It creates an even
playing field where you and your partner
(and your individual experiences) are given
equal weight in terms of importance and
value.

2. Humility deepens trust and emotional
safety by letting your partner know that you
do not think you are better than him/her.
When humility is speaking through us, the
message to our partner is: Your feelings and
reactions are just as important to me as my
own.

It's easier to turn to someone who is humble for comfort and support, versus someone who believes that your feelings are of little consequence. In this way, the pillar of humility allows the pillar of openness/presence to take hold by making your partner's experience central to your life.

3. Intimate relationships require us to be vulnerable. Intimacy (both emotional and sexual) can only be realized when we express the parts of ourselves that few others see. Shared humility allows you and your partner to relate to one another in more vulnerable ways by establishing a judgment-free zone; in essence, the message is, "We're two imperfect individuals who need to be accepted and loved for our imperfections (not in spite of them)."

4. Even the most loving couples fall victim to cycles of defensive indignation from

time-to-time. When we are hurt by the one we love, we can get pretty angry and either go into attack mode or retreat in an effort to distance ourselves from the source of the hurt.

However, you don't want defensiveness to hijack your marriage. This is where humility can be helpful. Humility and ongoing indignation cannot coexist. The intention to be humble brings you back from the whirlwind of defensive-anger, setting you gently down on the playing field of mutuality.

5. Humility enhances open-mindedness. Think of the people in your life (past and present) whom you really admired. Were they arrogant know-it-alls (arrogance breeds closed-mindedness), or were they humble in how they approached life? (Humility enhances open-mindedness.) Humility fosters an open-mindedness to new experiences. It positions you as a life-long learner, and when we relate to our partner in this way, we remain open to their uniqueness and self-evolution.

It's important to note that you can be humble and still feel confident in your life. You can practice humility and feel justified being upset or angry with your partner over some particular issue.

Humility shouldn't override your experiences that need validation. Be angry if anger is justified; assert your needs as vigorously as you need to in order to get your partner's attention; celebrate your victories and successes (as well as your partner's); feel good about yourself and your accomplishments; go after what's important to you...

You can do all of this while also relating to your partner (and others) with humility.

Celebrating your accomplishments doesn't mean you have to define yourself by them. Being angry with your spouse because s/he messed up doesn't mean that his/her concerns are no longer important. Feeling good about yourself shouldn't be fed by the shortcomings of others.

## Hop off the seesaw

You may think that there's no place for humility in your relationship. Actually, to take that one step further, you may think that there's no need for humility in your marriage.

Think again.

You might recognize that humility has a place in your professional life (when you have to—at times—face losing, and therefore have to learn how to lose with grace), or maybe in your friendships, since your friends wouldn't tolerate arrogance for too long before they'd tell you to hit the pavement. Perhaps you assume that you don't need to think about humility at all when it comes to your spouse because you don't ever behave in an arrogant way with him/her. "Plus," I've had clients say to me, "my marriage is the one place where I can totally be myself and not pretend to be okay with something when I'm not. So if I'm not a

humble person, why do I have to act like one
with my spouse?"

Here's where an exploration of the nuances
of humility can be helpful, including how
subtly the lack of humility may be working
against your union. And as is the case with
all the pillars for a lasting marriage, I
urge you to resist the common trap of
resigning yourself to an innate level of
these characteristics and therefore
remaining helpless to increase them. It's
not that some people are more naturally
humble than others; it's that some people
are choosing humility more often than
arrogance. Once you're aware that these
mindsets are choices and not pre-determined
traits like height or eye color, you can
make your own choices.

Humility can help us stop in our tracks
and question our "I'm right, you're wrong"
mindset. In this regard, humility acts as a
counter-balance to a rigid self-perception.
It acknowledges that no matter how clearly
you think you see a circumstance, event, or
person, there's another way of looking at

it. And your way isn't necessarily the best one.

Remember Russell and Lana from chapter one? Over and over again, they were arriving at the same impasse about money. Russell couldn't realize that Lana was motivated by anxiety (rather than a need to control him or rob him of pleasure) until he managed to put himself in her shoes the best he could. Yes, that requires empathy, but it requires something else, too: humility.

After that *ah-ha!* moment in my office, Russell and Lana went on to earnestly work on their issue around money. A few weeks later, we discussed their progress.

"You know," Russell said to me, "you weren't kidding about learning what was at the root of our problem being just the first step. Working on it has been *hard* some days."

"But it's worth it," Lana said. And then she frowned softly. "Wouldn't you say so, Russ?"

"Oh, God, yes. Totally worth it. Still, though, we've had some fights that have left me exhausted."

"*Discussions*," Lana corrected. "They were discussions. Maybe they were heated at times, though."

I asked for some details about their 'discussions' to get the sense of whether they were productive. Both agreed that they were. We talked about how couples often assume that conflict is always a bad sign, but that instead, conflict in marriage is inevitable. Getting stuck in a cycle of unresolved or escalating conflict can be a warning sign, not conflict in general. And often, when you're working *through* a problem (as Russell and Lana were), the conflict can appear to worsen before it gets better. But productive arguing (which includes staying on the topic at hand; not accusing or blaming or insulting the other; and actively listening to and acknowledging your partner's point, even when you're still quite sure of your own) can bring about desired change.

"The thing is," Russell said, "I was raised to see the man as the primary breadwinner. I know that's crazy, really, and I know that Lana and I make practically the same now, and she'll probably surpass me before too long, and I'm fine with that, really..." His voice trailed off before it picked back up. "But when Lana suggested we get separate bank accounts, it felt like I was failing as a man somehow."

"I thought it would make me feel less anxious," Lana explained. "If Russ wanted to buy things that would normally freak me out, I wouldn't have to watch the balance drop on the same account that the mortgage payments get drawn from. I'd have a 'safe' account for the bills."

"I mean," Russell said, "it makes sense on paper, but I guess I got scared. Separate accounts? What's next? Separate bedrooms? Separate houses?"

At first, Russell's fears were so difficult to look at for him that he looked the other way (as so many of us do when we're faced with painful emotions).

Initially he didn't even recognize it as fear at all, but instead was angry with Lana; he thought her arrangement was a different way of taking something away from him, as if her suggestion implied he wasn't worthy of being with her in every way. It was Lana's turn to put herself aside for a bit so that empathy and humility could come through and so that she could consider where Russell was coming from without defensiveness or feeling attacked. That allowed them to gently shine a light on Russell's reaction together, and get to the heart of what was troubling him.

"Finally, I had to find some humility," Russell said. "I couldn't complain about the belt around the bank account being tightened *and* complain when Lana offered me an account where I could deposit my checks and use a chunk of them for discretionary spending."

"You really think it needed humility?" Lana asked her husband.

"Sure," he said. "It took me a long time to admit this, but when I was so upset about not getting to spend money the way I wanted,

I was basically having a tantrum."

I hadn't ever thought of couple conflict in terms of 'tantruming' before. I asked Russell to go on.

He laughed. "Tantrums aren't just for kids. Just because I wasn't throwing anything or punching the wall, I was having a fit over not getting my way. And to me, that's real arrogance. That's saying, 'I know what's best and you don't, so just get out of my way and let me do what I want.' That's not who I want to be. When we got married, I traded in 'I' for 'us.' That means I don't always have the right answer, or the only answer."

When Russell was talking about humility, he wasn't positioning himself as someone who was doing something wrong. Rather, he was acknowledging that his "I'm right, you're wrong" mindset was shutting down communication, and therefore grinding everything to a halt. What humility did in this case was open a portal to the possibility that Lana's perspective had value and therefore should be listened to.

It took them off the seesaw of "if I'm up, you have to be down," and instead created a space where an alignment could occur between them.

## The bond between empathy and humility

Many couples that come to see me tell me that they've already figured out what they need: "We need to learn how to communicate effectively." So they're looking for tips and tools that specifically speak to communication. While this may be an important part of what they are needing, what is also frequently at play has little to do with communication and more to do with a lack of humility—a lack that creates a barrier to true connection between them.

You've probably heard the mantra of empathic understanding, "walk a mile in my shoes." Central to empathy is the ability to put your feelings, opinions, and perspectives aside to the degree that this is possible and once these are cleared away, attempt to wedge yourself into another's experience. See and experience the world through the eyes of another, especially if you are about to judge this person. As writer Charles D'Ambrosio so eloquently puts it: "...first you sympathize, then you judge—that's the complex human response. You sympathize first, and until that happens, you don't understand anything."

Practicing empathy in this way can interrupt the negative cycles of communication that might be consuming your relationship.

But this type of empathic listening isn't always easy to achieve, especially when you have strong feelings that are verging on defensive indignation (the **I'm totally right and how dare you challenge me?** stance that many of us are all too familiar with). Strong emotions have the potential to keep us internally closed off to the opinions and viewpoints of another.

As Russell pinpointed, empathy isn't possible without humility.

It's as if we have an internal airstrip

ready to receive our partner's message, and once the message safely lands, it can be examined and considered, and if needed, we may adjust our behavior accordingly. But there are times when our emotional reactions shut down the airstrip (due to an emotional blizzard, if you will) and as a result, all incoming messages are turned away. Keeping ourselves open during this intense internal weather is the challenge we all face. And there are those moments, after some time has passed and we've settled, that we slowly create an inner clearing so that our partner's message can be received.

As Russell showed us, regulating our emotions is just part of what is needed for true empathy. The other skill that we need to practice is humility. Humility, to be humble, is to let go of any feelings of superiority or importance. Why is it necessary to humble yourself in this way?

Without humility, empathy simply becomes a rote exercise that couples practice, an exercise that never takes root in the relationship landscape. I've seen this occur time and time again. All too often, couples practice empathy in my office in a very mechanical way, never really allowing themselves to "feel" the other's experience, at some level insisting on seeing their own perspective as superior (and therefore as *the* priority) even as they try to envision what their partner is going through.

This pseudo-empathy is a house of cards that collapses sooner or later and as a result, the couple is back to their defensive dance, a dance occurring to the dissonance of misunderstanding and not feeling listened to.

But when we practice humility, we start to feel that our experience is no more legitimate or truthful than our partner's. When we humble ourselves in this way, a new world is opened to the relationship. A new dance starts to occur, one with beautiful music in the background instead of harsh dissonance. A relationship pattern that is based upon true listening; true curiosity for the other's experience; a true openness to how you are impacting one another. This, of course, sounds good on paper, but it is difficult to practice at times—especially during conflict and during those times when we feel justified in our anger and hurt.

But here's something to consider: Your partner may feel equally justified in his/her feelings at the same time that you are basking in your indignation. This is why negative cycles become so intractable—you are both absolutely certain that the other is being unreasonable (and that your subjective truth is more justified than the other's). Here is where humility comes in—you dismount from your defensive high horse to understand that your partner feels just as mistreated or misunderstood as you do.

### Are you ready to practice humility and empathy?

Remember, humility starts with you; don't wait for your partner to show humility in order to respond in kind. Set the humility pace rather than following your partner's lead, and you will become responsible for creating a relationship that welcomes humility, empathy, emotional connection, and meaningful communication.

## Arrogance may be louder (and flashier) than humility, but humility will always see you home

You may think that because you don't use verbal put-downs or strut around in a beret and leather pants and croon, "I'm too sexy for you" to your partner, that you're never the least bit arrogant in your marriage. But arrogance in an intimate relationship is often much more subtle than it appears elsewhere.

Although there are varying degrees of arrogance (like all human dynamics, it runs on a continuum), arrogance sends messages like: *You need me more than I need you, so we're going to do things the way I want*; and *I know what's best for us, you don't.* Arrogance can be seen in false listening, where you know you're not really listening to your mate but you pretend anyway and send your mind elsewhere (this is different from distracted listening, where you may genuinely be trying to absorb what your partner is saying, but you're anxious about something, and those fearful thoughts are stealing some of your attention).

Even in its subtle forms, arrogance closes you down to the fullness of what your partner needs in the moment, and therefore temporarily makes you a less loving and less responsive mate. And since you don't want to be an unloving, unresponsive spouse (I can say that with assurance because you wouldn't be reading this book otherwise), choosing arrogance more and more will take you farther and farther from "home," in this case the home base of who you want to be as a partner.

Too often people think that being humble means being a doormat. Not at all! Practicing humility in your marriage does not mean eschewing self-care. It does not mean becoming a sieve through which your own needs escape, unfulfilled, while your partner's needs drown you. You can still be *confident* and be humble. You can't be *arrogant* and be humble, though. Arrogance and humility cannot co-exist in the same moment.

You may have heard the ancient Greek adage, "Be kind, for everyone you meet is fighting a hard battle." This is another example of humility and empathy working in concert. Empathy is required to imagine another's plight, but empathy requires humility to be realized. If you're coming from a place of arrogance, you'll think *your* battle is the hardest. You won't leave room for the potential of someone else's suffering.

And yes, thinking you've got it worse than anyone else is a form of arrogance. A very subtle, insidious form. It may look like self-deprecation on the surface (and therefore be mistaken for a type of humility), but down deep, it's a way of elevating yourself above others, even if the "elevation" takes the shape of *I've got it worse than everybody*. It sets you apart. It makes you different. It grants you "victory" in a competition of suffering. It's another shape that the distancing, anti-relationship mindset of arrogance takes. Also, it's important to note that humility is *not* self-deprecation. Humility is the admission that you don't know everything, and therefore it makes room for another's perspective.

Humility doesn't pierce your self-identity with the arrows of disparagement.

People often mistake humility for powerlessness. Quite the contrary, humility is a gentle means of claiming your power: the power to be proactive instead of reactive, the power to perceive a situation from more sides than your own, the power to be happy rather than "right," as well as the power of human beings to connect with fellow humans in the most meaningful of ways.

So when you're ready to leave arrogance and come home to the truth of who you are and to what you want your marriage to be, humility is the vehicle you'll choose to take you there.

## Questions to take you further:

1) To deepen your connection to humility even further, it can be helpful to think of someone you've admired who exemplified a humble approach to life. What specifically did you admire about this person? Note in particular how this person's humility was not a weakness, but rather a type of strength. You may have noticed a quiet self-confidence in this person (people who are truly humble have nothing to prove to others). For instance, many people see the Dalai Lama as an exceptionally humble person. And yet, he does not exude weakness, but rather, a quiet, non-intrusive strength.

Describe how strength or self-confidence revealed itself in the person you admire and then explain how you might like to emulate it.

2) We've made a connection between empathy and humility. Think about your own struggles in trying to be more empathic, and make room for the possibility that a lack of humility

might have prevented you from moving forward.

The next time your partner is in distress and needs you to listen, what can you do to get your own preconceived notions out of the way and truly be there for him/her? This will especially be important if your spouse is upset with you and needs you to hear how you've disappointed or frustrated him/her. In this instance, it will be very easy to get defensive. This is why practicing humility (and embracing it well *before* the conflict arises) is essential.

3) Because humility is an abstract concept, and, like all pillars it is a mindset (which means that practicing it begins on the level of your thoughts and decisions), it can be helpful to think about specific thoughts that you might try on that will bring more humility to your life.

What are some thoughts that will allow you to feel more humble? For instance: "Even though I don't understand why my wife is upset in this moment, this doesn't mean that her reaction is wrong." Or: "I would never have done what my husband just did, but that doesn't mean that he didn't have his reasons for doing it." Think of some examples in your own interactions with your mate where humility would've been a better response than arrogance or defensiveness. And think of your own narrative that you might use in future marital conflicts.

# 5. OPENNESS/PRESENCE

"My presence speaks volumes before I say a word." ~Mos Def

"An open heart is an open mind." ~The Dalai Lama

**Meet Tonya and Phil**

By all standards, Tonya and Phil have a solid relationship. In the whirlwind that is their lives, they manage to communicate the essentials of running a household, keeping up with the responsibilities of their two kids, while each holding down a full-time job outside the home. As Tonya said to me in one of our first couples counseling sessions, "We're actually a great team. We work well together on so many levels, and yet I feel something is missing."

Phil nodded his head in agreement.

"The teamwork is essential to our lives," Tonya went on, "but it almost feels like we're business partners instead of a married couple."

"That's not to say that we don't have sex," Phil added sheepishly. "We find the time for that here and there."

"Yeah, but it's the intimacy that I think is suffering," Tonya said. "It feels like when we talk or when we spend time together in general, we're just skimming a rock over the surface of the lake. We address what we need to in terms of what has to get done, but we're not going deeper, and that feels like a loss for me. But I don't know what to do about that."

The issue that Tonya and Phil are struggling with has to do with the willingness and ability to create a psychological space between them that would allow emotional connection to unfold. And it's not only couples with hectic lives that struggle with this issue. Because part of the dynamic of long-term relationships involves becoming comfortably familiar with one another, it's common that intimate communication on a deep level gets subsumed under the complacency that familiarity breeds.

The communication that feeds emotional connection involves a psychic turning toward one another, a clearing of the life clutter and the mental chatter that so often gets in the way of intimate connection. One of the things that we need to ask ourselves is: are we actively structuring our lives in an effort to avoid deeper levels of intimacy? Or is this an issue of a lack of knowledge? In other words, is the problem that you and your partner are not aware that you need to create a space that will foster deeper intimacy?

I asked Tonya and Phil if they would be open to trying a little experiment. I suspected that they had become so used to their time together being a means to an end (i.e., delegating child-care arrangements and various household tasks) rather than a way to celebrate their connection, that they could use some restructuring of time and focus in order to rebalance and realign.

What follows is the exercise I offered them, one they accepted. I encourage you and your partner to try it too.

## Create and safeguard a special space for your relationship

There are certain relationship skills that couples need in order to build and maintain a healthy marriage. An often-neglected—yet vital—skill involves your *imagination* and your ability to focus.

As the frantic pace of life continues to deplete the life-energy of couples, it has become more imperative than ever to build relationship buffers—protected moments that will allow you and your partner to retreat to a quiet place in order to nurture your love.

The following exercise is geared toward helping you and your partner learn to manage the distractions in your life. Being emotionally present with your partner is a prerequisite for so many essential parts of a healthy relationship: Effective communication, emotional intimacy, passion and sex, and mutual support and validation.

The first step is to carve out a certain amount of time together devoid of any and all distractions (this can be as short as fifteen minutes).

*But your physical presence does not guarantee your psychological/emotional presence.*

That's why the next step is essential.

Now use your imagination and pretend that nothing and no one else exists except your spouse/partner during this time. This needs to be a repetitive and deliberate act. During this time repeat to yourself, "No one and nothing else exists. I'm with the person

I want to be with and in this moment all I want to do is intensely focus on everything about him/her. Everything I need is right in front of me."

While carrying out this exercise you may find it helpful to focus on a particular aspect of your partner, like hair or eye color, or the sound of his/her voice. Note some feature that you haven't given attention to in a while, describing it to yourself in as much detail as possible. In this moment of alone-time try to see your partner in a new way. Don't worry if you have trouble doing this at first.

*Practice and keep at it.*

It's important to note that if you're used to communicating at the surface level (and Tonya's rock-skimming-the-lake analogy is a good one), then likely you will need some transitioning time from the frenetic world to a quiet, undistracted place where you only see your mate. Be kind to yourself around this—our busy world makes these types of focusing exercises challenging at first. (So don't beat yourself up if the first attempt or two doesn't go the way you'd like it to.)

Keep at it—the potential payoff to the depth and quality of the communication in your relationship will be well worth the initial antsy squirming you might experience when you're first temporarily unplugged from demands and distractions. And of course, it's not just the communication aspect of your relationship that you'll be nurturing—it's the emotional intimacy between you and your mate as well.

Couples report that the more they practice this (and similar) exercise(s), they start to feel their emotional connection deepen—a connection that carries over into other parts of their relationship.

After coming back to see me a few weeks after I'd introduced this exercise to Tonya and Phil, Tonya had this to say:

"It took us some time to get into the

space this exercise demands. But Phil and I talked about how it did create something different between us. Maybe something that we thought we'd lost once we had kids and stressful jobs. So we decided to keep trying it, and I'm so glad we did. We were pleasantly surprised by the direction our communication took. We reminisced, we looked ahead, we laughed. And it reminded me what a great listener Phil is."

This protected-space exercise is all about nurturing your authentic presence in your relationship, which is the gateway to meaningful connection.

"But what if my partner refuses to do this exercise with me?" you might be asking.

Not to worry—although this exercise is designed for couples, you can choose to be more open and more present for your partner (and therefore within your relationship overall) without saying a word about it to your mate. Your enhanced, "attuned" presence will be noticeable, even if your spouse can't put a finger on what's different about you. And there's a good chance that s/he will be positively impacted by that and will gradually become more open and present too.

The important thing to hold onto is your own motivation (rather than trying to force your partner's; no meaningful relationship change can come from coercion). After all, you can drag a spouse to a couples exercise, but you can't make him/her embrace it!

## Are you an emotionally attuned listener?

I witnessed a noteworthy conversation the other day between two women friends that I believe is relevant for couples. Yes, you could say I was eavesdropping, but when I see this kind of effective communication happening, I can't help myself. The setting was a busy coffee shop on a Saturday morning.

One of the women was upset about something and she clearly needed someone to talk to. What struck me is what this woman's friend did. She didn't offer any magical words, no grand wisdom, no packaged solutions or suggestions about what direction her distressed friend should take. In fact, from an outsider's perspective, it might look like she did very little, but this simply wasn't the case.

The power of what this woman offered her distressed friend had to do with emotional presence. It's hard to put this into words without it sounding like little more than good eye contact. It went way beyond this. From the next table, I could feel this woman's presence as she sat with her friend. Here is the best way I can describe the gift of listening she gave her companion:

• She was fully immersed and attuned to what her distressed friend was experiencing;

• She remained emotionally open to her friend's pain throughout the discussion;

• Her subtle body language (touching her friend's arm, nodding, tilting her head as she listened) offered powerful connecting moments;

• The few words she did use reinforced the

fact that she was totally with and present for her friend ("I'm here for you"; "Yes, I can see that"; "Please let me know how I can help you").

In short, this woman was emotionally attuned to her friend's experience and this attunement unfolded and organically flowed. This is what parents naturally do for their children when they're upset, and the research shows that this kind of emotional resonance (which in no way has to be perfect) leads to a sense of emotional security and the expectation that others are (or can be) available in ways that matter to you.

The truth is that it's difficult to teach this type of emotional attunement, but what's important for couples to hold onto is that we often unwittingly stand in the way of being present for our partner in this manner—it's as if we block our innate ability for emotional presence by thinking we have to do something "more" for the person who is upset (take away his/her pain; offer sage advice on which decision to make). This is a mistake because it keeps you outside of the other person's emotional orbit, and that distance between you will work against a strong emotional connection.

If I had to sum up the one thing this woman offered her distressed friend, it's this:

*The friend felt less **alone** in her pain.*

This is a powerful gift because emotional pain is an inherently lonely experience. We often feel most alone and lonely when we're suffering in some way. And too often, couples compound each other's emotional pain, adding layers of pain onto pain, by failing to join with one another through the power of presence.

**Self-reflective moment**

Reflect on the following questions, first, on your own, and then, if it feels safe to do so, with your spouse:

- How can you be more emotionally present for your spouse?

- What are your blocks to deepening your emotional presence for your partner?

- How do you need your partner to be emotionally present for you?

## Does it feel like your partner doesn't really *see* you?

This complicated world presents many pitfalls for possible disconnects between individuals. Quite possibly, the dynamic that makes us feel most alone is when we no longer feel seen and understood by the ones we love. That is a painful place indeed.

Both literally and metaphorically, the process of experiencing ourselves through the other—as being truly seen by a trusted loved one—allows us to connect with the deepest, most vital parts of ourselves. When we don't feel seen we either raise the stakes in order to be seen or we begin to hide as a means of self-protection.

The couples who come to see me for therapy do so for a variety of stated reasons. But a common thread throughout their distress is the experience of disconnection, a falling away from each other that arises from chronically being unseen or unacknowledged. Their breakdowns in communication, the "nagging" and arguing that twists them into emotional knots, the defensive walls that further the distance between them, all seem to melt away (at least momentarily) when one or both feel understood.

The origin of this need is captured in the following words by psychoanalyst and pediatrician D.W. Winnicott:

*"The mother gazes at the baby in her arms, and the baby gazes at his mother's face and finds himself therein..."*

Do you really "see" your partner?

*How can you put this into practice?*

Firstly, it's a process rather than a one-

or two-time event. Seeing and experiencing each other needs to continuously unfold, and when you hit a bump in the road, this unwanted detour needs to be acknowledged to allow you both to get back on track.

Secondly, this process isn't easy, because if it were, we'd all be effortlessly doing it. Part of the emotional rush associated with the newness of a relationship has to do with the excitement of mutual discovery—a mutual show-and-tell of sorts. Early on in your marriage, you might have found yourself being more open (sharing more of your experiences and reactions with your partner) as well as being more attentive to the process of acknowledging his/her shared experiences. In short, you both felt seen by each other (because you openly shared more of yourself and because you were more attentive and receptive to each other's sharing).

You and your partner cannot simultaneously hide and be seen. If you are withholding parts of yourself, segregating certain experiences from your spouse, the question to ponder is why this is occurring:

• Why are you not allowing yourself to be fully seen and experienced by him/her?

• Does it not feel emotionally safe to take the risks needed to be vulnerable with one another?

• Do you think your partner would say that you make him/her feel safe enough to be open and seen by you? Why or why not?

Establishing the relational conditions needed for the two of you to be emotionally open and vulnerable is essential to the process of seeing/experiencing each other. And this starts with a discussion. Talk about what you each need in order to be deeply knowable to one another (or to continue to be knowable). If you believe these conditions are currently lacking in your marriage, why do you think this is the case? Share this without blaming, without finger-pointing, and without the biting sting of defensiveness or accusation.

## The power of expressed interest

When I encourage this type of dialog with couples, they frequently share that they no longer feel that the other is interested in them any longer. "He just doesn't care" or "She doesn't seem to like what I talk about" is their pained refrain. Of course there will be topics and issues your partner discusses that you find uninteresting or worse, maybe even annoying. You won't find everything you each share fascinating. This is a fact of life and should be understood as such.

But it's a very different experience to feel lethargic over a particular topic your partner feels the need to discuss versus losing interest in him/her *as a person*. When we lose interest in our partner in this way, the excitement about who they are and what they feel and think falls away.

Beyond love and concern, it is expressed interest that creates the bridge required for connection. Genuine interest motivates us to see and experience our partner, and allows us to be open and present for them in a way that will strengthen the marital bond. (We will talk more about this in the next chapter as we explore the pillar of enthusiasm/curiosity.)

When we only reach for our partner when we're concerned about him/her or when we feel our relationship is in some kind of trouble, then worry becomes the central motivator for seeing and experiencing the other. When this is the case, once your reaching out placates your partner's distress or your worry about the relationship, the danger is that you'll fall back to an indifference default position that will again be felt by your partner.

We need to be seen and experienced throughout the relationship, not just when there are marital or relationship problems demanding our attention.

Before wrapping up the discussion of openness and presence, here is a question I suggest you and your partner explore together (if it feels safe to do so):

*What does it feel like to be deeply seen and known by each other?*

## Questions to take you further:

1)  You've probably heard that you can't love someone if you don't love yourself first. Do you agree with that? Why or why not?


Extrapolate that onto our discussion of openness and presence. Do you think you can be open to your spouse if you're not fully open to (or present for) yourself? How do you think a genuine openness to oneself looks? Do you think you are emotionally present for yourself much of the time, or do you think you have work to do in terms of allowing yourself to fully unfold and accept all the parts revealed?


2)  What are some emotional reactions you are prone to that could potentially get in the way of you being an open/present partner for your spouse? Can you identify these so that they have less control over your ability to be more emotionally available to your mate?

3)  If you find that your partner is reacting to you in ways that shut you down (for example, if you feel judged by him/her), how can you effectively communicate your feelings about this in a non-accusatory way? What do you think you're needing from your partner in those moments? And what do you think you're needing from *yourself* in those moments?

# 6. ENTHUSIASM/CURIOSITY

"Nothing great was ever achieved without enthusiasm." ~Ralph Waldo Emerson

"The first and simplest emotion which we discover in the human mind is curiosity." ~Edmund Burke

## Meet Sid and Nancy

Sid and Nancy attended one of my workshops on intimacy for couples a few years back. At that point, they'd been married for 36 years. What stood out for me was hearing that they attended workshops and seminars not because something was wrong with their relationship, but because they enjoyed nurturing an already-strong marriage. "Most

of all," Nancy said, "we love being life-
long learners. Even when things are going
well, we figure there's got to be valuable
stuff we can pick up along the way."

During the workshop, other participants
were drawn to Sid and Nancy, and before long
they took on an unofficial "mentor" role
with the other couples. We were all curious
about what they saw as attributing to the
success of their union.

"Well," Sid said thoughtfully when the
question was posed to him, "if I had to
choose one thing about what's made our
marriage strong for all this time, I'd have
to say it's that we have stayed *curious*
about each other."

Nancy quickly agreed. "We make it a point
to be interested in one another. And that's
why we make it a habit to ask each other
questions, even about small things, like
what we're each reading or what we thought
of the movie we just watched. We've known
couples who figure that after they've been
together for a long time, they can fill in
the blanks about their partner by assuming

and predicting. We try not to fall into that trap. For me, assuming is the polar opposite of the curiosity that Sid mentioned."

Sid jumped in. "When Nancy asks me questions about what I'm thinking and feeling, it challenges me to really explore my own reactions to particular things. Early on, I decided to consciously be different from my father, who only seemed to answer my mother's questions with a shrug or a mumbled, 'It's fine, dear.' I remember how much that seemed to frustrate my mother. Being enthusiastic about Nancy, and knowing she's enthusiastic about me and what matters to me, has not only expanded my life overall, it's cemented a connection between us."

For this couple, mutual curiosity is an essential marker on their pathway to connection. And they go out of their way to nurture this curiosity mindset (not only through taking classes and attending workshops together, and remaining engaged with and enthusiastic about the other, but also by maintaining individual pursuits and then coming back together to share what they learned and experienced).

As Sid mentioned, it would've been easy to fall into relationship patterns modeled by his father. When we show our partner that we are curious and enthusiastic about them (their interests, their hobbies, their job, their friends, their thoughts and feelings, etc.), we send the message, You matter to me, and I get excited about learning about you. Nancy hit on something extremely important when she described assumption as the antithesis to curiosity. When we do more assuming than learning about our partner (no matter how long we've been together), we slam the door on curiosity and enthusiasm.

You are continually growing and evolving. Your partner is too. So keep the fires of enthusiasm and curiosity burning!

## The benefits of nurturing curiosity and enthusiasm

One of the most ironic and painful aspects of marriage or long-term romantic relationships is that couples can be together for many years, spend a great deal of time together, yet ultimately know relatively little about one another. (A wife in marriage counseling once admitted that it felt like she knew more specifics about a character on her favorite TV show than about her own husband.)

Mutual curiosity is a frequent part of new love and romance, but all too often curiosity and enthusiasm about each other are replaced by *complacency* as couples reach a certain getting-to-know-you plateau and assume they know everything they need to about the other.

***There is a significant relationship cost when mutual curiosity is lost.***

In his research on successful relationships, John Gottman, Ph.D., found that couples who have detailed and up-to-date information about each other (what Dr. Gottman calls a *Love Map*) are more likely to feel closer (experience deeper emotional intimacy) and are more likely to weather the inevitable relationship storms that occur from time to time. Regularly updating your Love Maps goes a long way to keeping your marriage healthy.

## How comprehensive is your Love Map of your spouse?

Couples who make an effort to keep up with the details of each other's life report feeling more cared for and central to one another—as a husband recently shared, "I feel like I matter, like I'm important when Cindy asks me about my friends, my work or my views about certain issues. If she never asked, I guess I'd just assume she didn't care all that much about me."

## Strengthen your marriage through *ongoing* curiosity and enthusiasm

The first (and often most important) step
is to hit the pause button on any
assumptions and thoughts you may hold that
block you from approaching your partner with
a curious, open mindset.

Challenge any assumptions that take the
following form: "I already know everything
there is to know about him, case closed";
"There are no more surprises between us, we
know each other so well"; "I know her better
than she knows herself." These and similar
thoughts will prevent the cultivation of
mutual interest and the necessary curiosity
that is part of a healthy marriage.

Remember, the goal is to maintain an
exploration of each other's evolving
interests, dreams (realized and unrealized),
deepest fears, etc. You might feel you know
everything there is to know about your
partner at one point in time, but you and
your partner are both always evolving, so
there will always be something new to
discover.

The next step is to develop a series of questions to ask each other (even if you believe you already know how your partner will respond)-often it is the process of asking and responding that allows for the deepening of emotional intimacy. These can be simple, playful questions (such as, "What is your favorite food?"; "List your three favorite movies") and more serious questions (such as, "What is your biggest regret in life?"; "If you could change one thing about yourself, what would it be?"; "What is a dream that you'd like to have realized?"). Start here or be creative and come up with your own questions that feel meaningful for the life that you and your partner share.

The final step is to share your lists of questions with each other and take turns answering each question. The goal of the listener is to be fully present and to take in the information that is being disclosed. If further questions spontaneously arise while discussing each other's answers, you can add them to the list or ask the questions as they come up.

This type of exercise will allow you each to keep up-to-date with one another while deepening the bond of emotional intimacy all at the same time. This is a win-win situation for your marriage!


## How well do you know your spouse?

*Are you a curious partner?*

All marriages evolve, and this evolution involves getting to know your spouse at a deeper level. Early in the relationship, this process moves along naturally and at its own pace—but as relationships mature, this process levels off, and the mutual curiosity that was once a regular part of a relationship vanishes.

*Why is that?*

Simple: over time we reach a certain level of transparency that ends up shutting down curiosity—couples end up believing that they know everything there is to know about each other. For many of us, this is quite comforting and brings a sense of stability to our relationship and lives.

But this can also lead to a rut. This is because emotional intimacy requires ongoing, mutual understanding, and since we are all continually evolving beings (growing and changing psychologically, physically, and spiritually), mutual curiosity needs to keep up with this evolution. This is the case no matter how long you've been together.

## 7 questions to pique curiosity in your relationship

Below are questions designed to help you think about your relationship (and your partner) in a new light. You might want to answer them separately or together as a couple, whichever works best for you. As you share your responses with each other, try to be open and curious about the nuances of one another's answers.

It's best to approach this exercise with a *beginner's mind* (in other words, let go of the preconceptions you hold about your partner).

(Please take your time answering these questions and come back to them as often as you like in order to deepen the journey of mutual discovery.)

1. Would you want to be your partner's friend even if you didn't have romantic feelings for him/her? Why? Why not? Based on your observations, what kind of friend is s/he to others?

2. How do others describe your spouse? How does s/he treat others in general (cashiers, waitstaff, coworkers, etc.)? Is this consistent with the type of partner s/he is to you?

3. Describe how s/he handles stress and demanding circumstances. What seems to help your partner during these trying times? What makes things worse?

4. If your partner won the lottery, how would s/he spend the money? Predict his/her first 5 purchases. Are these consistent with your values?

5. What are your spouse's greatest fears in life? How might these play out in your marriage?

6. What brings your partner the greatest joy? What makes him/her feel the happiest and the most fulfilled? What is your partner truly passionate about? Where does s/he find meaning in life?

7. If your spouse could magically change one thing about his/her life and solve a particular world issue/problem, what would those be and why?

Remember, don't assume you know how your

spouse/partner will respond—the goal isn't
to guess his/her answers but instead to be
open and curious about each other's evolving
and changing interests, passions and
viewpoints.

Even if you were able to predict 85-90% of
your partner's answers, that still leaves a
valuable chunk of information to explore.
That's where your enthusiasm and curiosity
energy should be focused.

You can use these questions as a way to
create greater emotional intimacy by
entering into a dialogue with your spouse
about her/his responses. And, in the spirit
of enthusiasm and curiosity, have fun doing
it!

**Questions to take you further:**

1) To be enthusiastic is to experience emotional abandon in the moment. Self-judgment, self-consciousness, and anxiety can all shut down enthusiasm. Identify any potential blocks that prevent you from getting enthusiastically caught up in your partner's life.

2) Asking questions about each other and about the particulars of the day is a powerful expression of curiosity. If this doesn't seem to come naturally to you, think of different questions you can practice asking of your partner, and notice which ones land and which ones fall flat.

3) Relationship complacency has the tendency to dampen curiosity and enthusiasm. Identify how complacency has impacted you in your marriage and make a plan to counter the inertia of feeling stuck in a rut. You may want to invite your partner to join you in co-creating a plan that you both can

implement.

# 7. GRATITUDE

"Gratitude is the heart's memory." ~French Proverb

**Meet Micah and Joelle**

"I know it sounds crazy," Micah said, "but the best thing that ever happened to me was when a truck hit my motorcycle and sent me to the hospital. I broke my collarbone, my leg in three places (I have a metal rod in my femur), and *both* arms." He shook his head and laughed bitterly. "And those are just the highlights. I also lost some teeth, permanently destroyed a bunch of skin by skidding on the pavement, had a concussion...*and* my bike was totaled."

How can Micah say this was the best thing that ever happened to him? Let's keep listening:

"When I woke up in the hospital, I knew I was lucky to be alive. *Really* lucky. Before then, I took most things for granted. Joelle is naturally a more appreciative person than I am, always seeing the glass half-full. But I tended to focus on things that needed to be fixed."

Joelle jumped into the discussion at that point. "We'd been married four years at the time of the accident, though we lived together for four more prior to marrying. And the whole time I'd been trying to get him to celebrate the good that we already had, rather than worry about the next bad thing that might be around the corner, or overly obsessing about problems that had to be resolved."

"That's true," Micah said. "But I wasn't getting it. I just figured that Joelle was born grateful, and that I couldn't be like her. But man, the accident was a massive wakeup call to me. I realized that there were only two ways to live: being grateful for the good things you already have, or taking the good things for granted while complaining about what you didn't have. And I didn't want to waste another day missing the good stuff. Not only in my life and in the world, but in our marriage."

The power of gratitude has been touted through the centuries by philosophers, spiritual leaders, and scholars. You have probably experienced its power firsthand in your own life. However, that doesn't mean it's always easy to hold onto within a relationship. There will inevitably be times when your partner does something that very much annoys you (and vice versa), and in those moments of flared tempers, it's hard not to get pulled into the cycle of negativity. In fact, the negative has a powerful pull on us, and can easily shape the course of a relationship...if we allow it to (or if we are unaware of it).

To counter the slide toward the negative, couples must make the conscious effort—the *choice*—to practice gratitude (yes, it is a practice, which means that it's available to all of us, not just a few of us born with a natural tendency toward appreciation...and you don't need to be involved in a major vehicular accident to take up the practice of gratitude and make it your go-to habit).

## Enhance your love through positive interactions

You're probably already aware of how important it is to be supportive when your spouse shares distressing news with you. If your husband calls you at work to tell you he just lost his job, I'm sure none of you would set the phone down while you finished eating your lunch (and while you could still hear him crying through the receiver).

But have you ever thought about how important it is to be supportive, attentive and *responsive* when your partner has *good* news to share? Research shows that it most certainly is. Shelly L. Gable, Ph.D., has studied the effects of positive interactions on intimate relationships. Dr. Gable notes that most of the research on relationships has focused on how couples respond to each other during stressful events.

When you listen to good news that your partner shares, it's important to respond in what Dr. Gable calls an *active and constructive* manner.

If your wife reports that she just became a partner at her law firm, and if you respond actively and constructively, you might say (with elation), "Honey, that's fabulous! All your hard work validated! What do you want to do to celebrate? Oh, and tell me all the details."

If you were to respond *passively*, you might barely look up from your newspaper, say, "That's nice, dear," and not show any excitement about the good news.

Active and constructive responses build intimacy, trust and relationship satisfaction. Supportive interactions around positive events are also associated with fewer daily conflicts. (*Read that sentence again, because that has big implications for every couple.*) And these types of interactions make up the gratitude pillar of intimacy, brick by brick.

When you respond in a supportive way to positive events in your spouse's life, you are highlighting your partner's strengths— the qualities that make him/her feel empowered and worthwhile. In essence, you are saying, "I am grateful for you and for our relationship, and I feel gratitude for the same things you are grateful for." When you affirm your partner's strengths, you make your partner feel better about himself/herself and the relationship.

**Positive interactions also enhance the resiliency of the relationship.**

So, if you want to strengthen your marriage, heighten your awareness to all of the positive events your partner experiences (even the smaller, less dramatic events).

When s/he shares positive news, respond in a way that validates and recognizes his/her experience.

Try it today, and then try to make it a regular practice. You'll be on your way to building a more satisfying and resilient relationship.

## Don't save gratitude for the big moments

If you tend to stop whatever you're doing to express dismay over something left undone or something done improperly, you're not alone. After all, humans are problem-solvers by nature. If we're faced with a situation that needs fixing, we're likely to fix it, or, if the problem is outside of our purview, to speak up about it.

"Didn't I ask you to repair that lock last week? I got locked out when I went outside to take the trash out!"; "I thought you said you were staying on top of the bills. We got two past-due notices today!"; "If you're not going to make the call to get us an appointment, at least say so so that I can do it."

Although the details will vary, chances are you've been at the receiving *and* delivering end of similar statements of frustration. Life is complicated and constantly moving. It's impossible to get everything done perfectly, no matter how we might try. So there will be times when we drop the ball or when we have to pitch in to fix a problem exacerbated by our partner missing something. And those times are the ones that tend to linger in our consciousness more than the smooth, uneventful times. (The squeaky wheel gets the grease, even within our own minds.)

Not only do we tend to remember crisis moments more vividly than non-crisis moments, but we also tend to be vigilant when it comes to trying to *prevent* those crises, so we're actively anticipating and looking for potholes in the road of life, even when we're driving on a perfectly smooth stretch of pavement.

All this is not said for you to feel resigned to the pattern of looking out for the brambles so intently that you never manage to smell the roses. Quite the contrary—when you bring this pattern to your awareness, you can understand why it's so common. That understanding, coupled with kindness to yourself, can sow the seeds of self-improvement and relationship improvement.

Research has consistently shown that people who take the time to feel grateful for the "little" things in their lives (even when they're facing major struggles) report a greater degree of happiness than people who solely focus on resolving problems when they arise. If a mindset of being thankful is good for an individual, it stands to reason that it is good for a couple. Quite often, love and gratitude go hand-in-hand.

If you start noticing all the things you're grateful to your partner for, and if you communicate those things to him/her, you *both* benefit.

But how can we make showing gratitude a habit when we're so immersed in living a fast-paced life that demands we put out fire after fire?

Incorporating ongoing appreciation into your relationship doesn't require a major upheaval of your life...but, as with anything worth doing, it takes consistency. Small steps are great; the key is to continue taking those little steps, day after day.

**5 tips for expressing appreciation in your marriage**

**1) Notice the good**

Even if you feel overwhelmed with all that you have to do (and overwhelmed with how much is left undone), there are most likely things you are grateful for regarding your life with your partner. The problem is that the demands of life are noisy and persistent and don't allow you to hear the appreciation that whispers underneath, even if it is appreciation for a tiny thing that might seem inconsequential in the face of all the "problems" clamoring for attention. (And keep in mind that noticing the good does not mean denying the trouble spots in life or your marriage. **Denial is *never* a beneficial** approach to intimate relationships.)

With practice, you can quiet the voice that reminds you of what hasn't gone right and can listen for the softer voice that tells you what is *already* right. (Keeping detailed "to-do" lists can help here; making lists can get the chores out of your head, so to speak, which keeps the chores or issues in place for dealing with later. This allows you to de-clutter your mind so you can be more grateful for the things that run smoothly.) And then you can notice what's working well between you and your partner, and can notice how your partner contributes to that.

## 2) Feel the gratitude

You can't express gratitude if you're not feeling it (well, you can, but it won't be true gratitude, and so it won't feel good to you or your partner). Too many people try to force themselves into being grateful, and the risk of that is you can end up resenting yourself and your partner down the road. Telling yourself you're grateful if you're not is nothing more than gratitude lip-service.

**Allow the *noticing* (which is an intellectual activity) to drop down to *feeling* (which** is experiential, and sometimes even beyond words). If you're not feeling it, don't force yourself or beat yourself up for that. Go back to noticing when you're ready and try again at a later time.

## 3) Say it

Noticing and feeling appreciation are beneficial for you as an individual, but you want to go further and have your marriage benefit, too. So you need to go from expressing the gratitude within yourself to expressing it to your partner. And this next point can't be stressed enough (so here it comes in bold): **Don't wait for a major event to occur to tell your partner you appreciate something that s/he has done.** Research shows that regular, consistent mentions of gratitude do more for a couple's closeness and mutual good will than infrequent ones.

Your partner will not tire of hearing you say, "I appreciated when you _____," so don't worry about the expression of gratitude losing its luster.

## 4) Write it

In addition to giving voice to the moments when you feel appreciation for something helpful your spouse did for you (or even for your partner in general, or some facet of him/her that you especially love), sending words of thanks via notes of gratitude are wonderful ways to cement this mindset in your life. Texts, emails, notes, surprise cards sent to his/her place of work show your partner that you really mean what you say. These don't need to be epic tomes or over-the-top...for instance, something as simple yet specific as this would be super: *Thank you for being so supportive the other night after my bad day at work—I appreciate how you took care of dinner and getting the kids to bed so that I could de-stress.*

Further, the act of writing something stimulates your brain so that you might come up with more to appreciate than you would've if you'd only spoken your thoughts. And the odds are, your partner will very much appreciate your appreciation too!

## 5) Repeat

This next point is a challenging one for many, but it is important for an authentic gratitude mindset to take hold in your marriage or relationship. And that is: *Don't express gratitude with the expectation that your partner must reciprocate.* If you only give appreciation because you're angling to get some from him/her, then in essence you're holding a healthy mindset hostage to something beyond your control.

You can't control whether your partner

expresses gratitude to you (though these types of things tend to be contagious, so it's likely you'll see some positive shifting along these lines). You can only control how you behave in the relationship (but your behavior can't help but impact the union overall). Focus on how you're feeling and what feels right to you, not on how you want your partner to behave in response.

So if you're feeling good about the "attitude of gratitude," go ahead and repeat the *noticing, feeling, saying, writing* that we discussed above, but first make sure that your only motive is to notice what's already working in your marriage or relationship and sharing that with your mate. If your motive is to get him/her to do the same for you, you've got some reassessing to do.

*Are you ready to make appreciation a regular part of your marriage?*

## Questions to take you further:

1) Like all the pillars, gratitude is a mindset that must be nurtured. To this end, start to actively identify the things about your spouse that you appreciate. You may want to write these down. And in particular, focus on the little things about him/her that you are grateful for.

(I once worked with a couple where the wife was determined to make gratitude a habit. She'd read that a habit takes 21 consecutive days to take root in your mind and in your life, so her plan was to write her husband a brief note about *one* thing she was grateful for about him each day and mail a different note to him at work for 21 days in a row.

The things she noted weren't huge, dramatic things about her husband, but rather, the smaller, steadier things that made up their daily lives. For instance, one note said: *I appreciate how you start the coffee every morning.* Another read: *I am grateful for the fact that you love to make me laugh and how you always seem to be thinking up new ways.* And another: *I feel gratitude for how you always, always thank me for fixing us a meal, even if I've only opened a can of soup.*

She said that she loved sending these "I'm grateful for" notes so much that she didn't stop at 21. She kept it up for an entire month, and she went on to say that that practice brought them closer than ever as a couple, and made gratitude a whole lot easier for her to feel in her life and her outlook on the world at large.)

2) It's easy for all of us to get pulled down by what isn't working with our partner. To counter this slippery slope, how can you create communication balance by letting your spouse know what isn't working when appropriate, while also focusing on the positives that already exist in your relationship? Remember, it's easy for positives to get subsumed under the weight of things that need fixing.

3) How can you and your mate create a shared space to communicate what you each appreciate about the other? Maybe this can occur during a weekly date night. Or in the evenings before bed. In either case, scheduling this time together is a good idea, because that is what will make it happen.

# 8. HONESTY

"Keep the other person's well-being in mind when you feel an attack of soul-purging truth coming on." ~ Betty White

## Let's talk truth

Couples in committed relationships expect their partner to be truthful in who they are, what they feel, what they share, and the like. The pillar of honesty implies that when it comes to your partner, what you see is what you get. There are no hidden corners, no closets down dark hallways concealing secrets that can ultimately hurt the relationship.

And, of course, honesty starts with your relationship to yourself. It is something you must bring to your partner to help make him/her feel secure and grounded in the relationship. Before discussing why you may be dishonest with your partner at times, let's turn our attention to why honesty is central to your marriage.

## 1) Honesty as a core value

We each enter our relationship with certain core values, beliefs that we've acquired throughout our lives that are central to our world view and who we are as people. While you may be fully conscious of the values that shape your life, some of them may have taken up residence in the unconscious part of your mind where they quietly mold your experiences.

For many, honesty is a central value. When this is the case, you may make an effort to be open and honest with your spouse (and others). You may react negatively when you discover someone has lied to you and you may go out of your way not to lie to others.

## 2) Honesty as an expression of authenticity

Authenticity is an ideal that many of us strive for—the desire to be genuine and honor our deepest truths. For authenticity to be realized, we must be honest with ourselves, we must know what we're feeling, understand what our true motivations are, as well as be aware of our own shortcomings.

Without such self-directed honesty, many of our attempts to be "authentic" can actually be defensive maneuvers that hide our struggles and vulnerabilities. In these instances, a short-sided arrogance is masquerading as authenticity. One of the most powerful authentic moments is to acknowledge your uncertainty and, if appropriate, ask for help.

However, authentic honesty shouldn't come at the cost of your partner's wellbeing. Tact and sensitivity should figure in in how you express yourself. In short, you can be real, you can be honest, and you can be genuine without being self-centered and insensitive. Remember the pillar of humility and the important communication skill of anticipatory empathy.

In order to develop a trusting, stable relationship with your partner, you must first decide to be honest. After all, think about what it would be like if the situation were reversed: Imagine how difficult life would be if you couldn't count on what your mate told you. If you feared your spouse usually handed you lies, your natural curiosity about his/her whereabouts or feelings could easily turn into suspicion and chronic doubt.

## 3) **Honesty as an expression of mutual commitment**

Marriage and intimate relationships rest on a foundation of mutual commitment. The particulars of commitment are negotiated from couple to couple, and often honesty (the absence of deceitfulness) is part of this commitment foundation.

Frequently this commitment is implied without being directly spoken. We assume that our partner is going to be faithful, that s/he is going to share the things that are important to him/her and follow through on the mutual obligations that are part of the shared life; and we except that our partner won't stockpile secrets that clearly violate the implicit commitment-honesty pact.

Honesty is clearly important and in my work as a psychologist, I have a front-row seat to the impact that dishonesty has on relationships. And the fact is, many of us aren't totally forthcoming at times with our partner. Understanding why this is can go a long way in making honesty a healthy part of your life and union.

The truth of the matter is that most of us fib to our partners now and then, and sometimes with good reason (at least we convince ourselves it's for good reason). But when lying becomes the norm rather than the exception, and when dishonesty stems from self-serving reasons only, the relationship suffers. Therefore, becoming mindful of the reasons why you might lie is important to the overall health and well-being of your marriage.

**Why you might not be so honest at times**

**1) Protecting your partner —"The little white lie"**

Wesley recently lied to his wife Maggie. A medical test detected a spot her internist was concerned about, so the doctor scheduled Maggie for further tests. Wesley sensed his wife's anxiety (and felt his own) and he attempted to present a calm emotional exterior to comfort her.

So when Maggie asked her husband if he was afraid the spot could be cancer, Wesley confidently responded, "Absolutely not. Breast cancer doesn't even run in your family!"

In truth, Wesley was a nervous wreck and

feared the worst. But denying his own fears
helped with his wife's escalating anxieties.
Would you withhold your honest feelings like
Wesley did if you were in his shoes?


## 2) Fear-based dishonesty

Fear is the basis for a significant
portion of lying that occurs in marriages.
By telling the truth, you fear some type of
reprisal from your partner—you might
anticipate a verbal attack, anger,
disapproval, belittlement, and/or
disappointment. When you imagine your
partner's reaction to your truth (whatever
that truth might be), you feel anxious and
as a result, withhold the truth or cover it
up in some way.

Couples prone to fear-based dishonesty
need to be careful because this can snowball
and before you know it, the emotional
connection that is so important to your
relationship can be compromised by your
fear-based decisions to withhold what is
going on with you.

## 3) Shame-based lying

What if you told the truth and someone's reaction caused you to feel ridiculed? Embarrassed? "Less-than"?

This is a pretty common event, especially in childhood. We can all probably recall witnessing instances of playground injuries ending in tears for one child and laughter and ridicule by the others. Such shaming reactions often leave an indelible psychic scar, especially in boys who are seen as somehow defective if they express vulnerable feelings.

Such experiences and the socialization of machismo can lead men to be "feeling-phobic." Twisting the truth becomes a method of protection against the anticipation of shaming reactions (this can occur even when your spouse has never reacted in a shaming way toward you). A significant portion of the men I work with in couples counseling are highly prone to feeling ashamed and as a result, lie in an effort to prevent themselves from being seen as vulnerable.

But, of course, shame-based dishonesty isn't the province of men alone. Women are all-too-familiar with being shamed by insensitive others. What's important is for all of us to understand the powerful self-shifting nature of shame and how the anticipation of rejection or ridicule (two common shaming experiences) can cause us to abandon our commitment to honesty.

## 4) Habitual dishonesty

Some habits die hard. And this is certainly the cause of habitual lying.

Habitual lying can take on a life of its own, and before you know it, you don't even realize you're not being honest. You've lied for so long, and across so many different circumstances, that it has become commonplace. A habit that is turning into a personality trait.

To habitually lie is to spin tales when there's no objective reason for deception.

Peel back the habitual liar's surface confidence and you'll find a beleaguered, self-doubting and confused individual.

You may have hidden for so long that the truth feels assaultive to your identity. In fact, truth and deceit have blurred to the point that it may be difficult to tease them apart. If this is the case, it will be important to set the daily intention to make honesty a part of your life and to make efforts to catch the knee-jerk moments when you start to twist the truth. This is the first and one of the biggest steps in reclaiming the gifts that can come with honesty.

## 5) Self-deception

The ability to deceive ourselves is quite remarkable. We all have psychological defenses that help us deal with stressful experiences, feelings that overwhelm us, thoughts and emotions that make us uneasy because they conflict with our self-image (with who we'd like to be). These same defenses allow us to ignore what we don't like about ourselves—creating a type of virtual reality that helps us to see only what we desire.

As self-deception increases, the tendency to be less than honest with your spouse also increases.

Chronic self-deception can pose challenges for your relationship, because intimacy demands that you share the deepest, most vulnerable parts of yourself. If you deny these parts of yourself, you will certainly refuse your partner access to these places. In these instances, you might be dishonest so that your partner doesn't see the parts of you that you don't even want to acknowledge.

By gaining an understanding of why you or your spouse might choose to be dishonest, you will be in a better position to prevent the dynamics of lying and secrecy from hijacking your marriage. The goal is to be mindful of why you aren't being honest and to overcome this pattern for the sake of your relationship.

While some degree of dishonesty in long-term relationships might be common (for instance, protecting your partner's feelings by telling a "white lie"), certain patterns of dishonesty always run the risk of damaging what you and your spouse have worked so hard to build together.

**Are you forsaking one pillar for the sake of another?**

Let's think back to Micah and Joelle from the previous chapter. Recall that it was after a brush with death that Micah reassessed his prevailing attitude about life and then chose a mindset of gratitude.

About a year after I spoke with them last, I got a call from Joelle asking for an appointment. After a handful of meetings with them, the following became apparent:

Micah's daily practice of gratitude had gradually faded and had given way to passive-aggressive behaviors at times, even as he was insisting that he was being thankful. He surprised me when he said, "It's really hard to show appreciation when Joelle does things that upset me. At first I was able to do that, but then it just seemed to get the best of me. Still," he added hastily, "I'm really grateful, I really am."

In essence, Micah started to use gratitude as a way to suppress a set of feelings he was experiencing in specific moments (as in when he and Joelle would have a disagreement). So he wasn't being honest with himself or with his wife when he would express appreciation in those times (or, more aptly, *pseudo-appreciation*) through clenched teeth. He abandoned the pillar of honest-authentic communication by saying one thing and meaning another.

Ideally, Micah could've done both: he could've given Joelle feedback that might've been an expression of his frustration or disappointment in the moment while still honoring his choice for gratitude. In other words, Micah didn't have to force himself (or Joelle) into believing that he was grateful for the exact thing she was doing or saying in order to continue to have a gratitude mindset overall. Being grateful does not mean denying things. Micah could've still been grateful for his marriage, for his wife, for the safe place they had created in which he could voice his opinions, while at the same time being tactfully and gently honest about how Joelle's behavior was pushing his buttons.

Earlier, we mentioned that arrogance and humility cannot co-exist in the same moment. That is not true for gratitude and honesty— they are not mutually exclusive thought systems. So if you need to take a time-out with your mate and say, "Hey, what you said at breakfast really hurt my feelings," that doesn't mean that in that moment you are not grateful for him/her and not grateful for the freedom to express your truth and be your authentic self within the relationship.

After a few sessions of working together, Micah went home with a plan for how to balance the pillars of gratitude and honesty. When it comes to implementing these pillars in your marriage, it's important not to cling to any one of them so tenaciously or so nearsightedly that you exclude the others. A meaningful relationship (and a meaningful life) is one that is balanced. While you may find one or two pillars more relevant than others at a particular time, it's a good idea to look back on them as time goes on to be sure you're strengthening them all.

When Micah began embracing the pillar of
honesty in a way that felt right for him, he
was able to see that being grateful didn't
need to feel like a burden—gratitude didn't
have to be perceived as something designed
to shut down his authentic reactions. He
discovered that he could continue to
experience deep appreciation for all the
good in his life while he was making space
for his truth within the larger space of the
marriage.

**Questions to take you further:**

Now it's time for some honest self-reflection to help you better understand the role of honesty/dishonesty in your marriage. Here are some questions to help you gain insight into the role that truth and lying might have in your marriage or relationship:

1) What role does honesty play in your life and relationship? How have you and your partner negotiated honesty in your commitment to one another?

2) Do you see yourself in any of the 5 reasons for being dishonest that were explored in the opening of this chapter? What steps can you take to overcome these patterns? What would you need in order to share with your spouse/partner the reasons you feel you have to withhold the truth?

3) Do you find yourself lying more often in your marriage as compared to past

relationships and other areas of your life? If so, why do you think this is the case? What steps can you take to change this pattern?

I use these questions when I work with someone who struggles with telling the truth to his/her loved ones. Don't rush through them; revisit them as often as you need in order to deepen your understanding of why you may withhold the truth. This is important information to have so that you can build (or rebuild) a relationship that is supported by the pillar of honesty.

## 9. WRAP-UP

One day a while back, when the idea for this book was just a lone, un-planted, un-watered seed, I was driving to work—not quite running late, but not with loads of time to spare, either—when I spotted a dog that seemed to be without an owner on the opposite side of the road. He looked lost.

Because I am very much a dog person, I pulled over and got out of my car. The dog's ears pricked as I ran across the road to him, and then his tail started wagging. At one point I worried he'd dash out in front of cars to get to me quicker than I was managing to get to him.

He looked like a yellow lab—he was a big, sweet, goofy dog, docile and friendly, and clearly lost. Luckily, he was wearing a collar with ID. I scratched him behind the ears while I read the tags. "Okay, Buddy," I said, "let's get you home."

I pulled my cell out of my pocket and called the phone number on Buddy's tag, waiting through ring after ring while holding tight to the dog's collar so he wouldn't wander away. No answer. And no voice mail. I tried a text but I wasn't sure I was calling a cell. The tag didn't include an address.

By this point, I was running the risk of showing up late for my first client session of the day, something I really did not want to do. My options ran through my head: Bring Buddy to the office (which wasn't ideal—my landlord didn't allow animals other than service animals into the small building since he has an office in there and is very allergic); call animal control and wait with Buddy (which would most definitely make me late); leave Buddy in the car in my office parking lot until animal control got there (no way, it was too hot for that). I didn't have time to drive home by this point, though it wouldn't be prudent to drop Buddy off with my two dogs and my wife not home anyway...I had no idea if they'd all get along or how Buddy would do trapped in a strange house.

I tried the phone number again (to no avail) and hoped an epiphany would strike as I moved my feet. Holding onto Buddy's collar, I crossed the street to my car with a bent back. As I made it to the curb, a car pulled up in front of mine. A woman burst out of the driver's seat before she even turned off the engine. A man got out of the passenger seat.

"Buddy!" she said, holding her arms wide. "There you are!"

Buddy's tail flicked even faster.

"Oh," I said, "is this your dog?"

"He sure is," the man said, surrounding Buddy in a hug that the dog seemed to eat up.

"I'm glad," I said. "I called the number but didn't get you. I was thinking about bringing him to my office so he wouldn't get hit by a car."

"Thank you," the man said. He held his hand for a shake while his companion hooked a leash onto Buddy's collar. "Louis."

I introduced myself in kind, with my first name.

"And this is my wife, Geena."

"I'm sorry to inconvenience you," Geena said. "We were visiting a friend and we thought he was in the backyard. He managed to get over the fence."

"No inconvenience," I assured them. "I'm glad you drove by. I've got to get going, though. I'm running late for work."

"Where do you work?" Geena asked.

"She'll probably bake you brownies to thank you," Louis said with an affectionate eyeroll. "Are you okay with chocolate?"

Geena laughed. "You know me, Lou."

"I love chocolate," I said, "but you really don't have to do anything to thank me. I'm just glad you're reunited with Buddy."

"It would make me feel good," Geena said. "Unless you don't want me to know where you work."

It was my turn to laugh. I told them where my office was, and Geena appeared to recognize the address. She said, "Do you happen to be Rich-the-couples-counselor?"

"I guess I am."

"Cool. We have friends who see you for counseling."

Louis jumped in. "Geen, he can't even admit he's seeing them. Patient confidentiality. Right?"

I nodded.

"Well," she went on, as she helped Buddy onto the backseat of the car, "they said working with you has been really great. I won't even mention their names so it doesn't have to be awkward."

"They've been talking about pillars," Louis said. "At first I thought they were telling us about some architecture class they were taking. But then they said their marriage counselor was the one with the pillars."

"Guilty as charged," I said.

"I like that metaphor," Geena said. "Louis and I don't have complaints, but I like to be proactive. So our friends have been sharing tips."

"We'd better let you get to work," Louis said. "Thanks for looking out for Buddy."

"And thanks for making a difference in our friends' marriage," Geena added.

"Something tells me that brownies are in your future," Louis said as I got in my car.

Geena swatted his arm playfully.

I was just barely on time for my first clients of the day (had just enough time to unlock my office and stick my lunch in the fridge in the back room before they arrived), but the interaction with Buddy and his people was worth the rushed feeling. It's always nice to hear from someone who doesn't have a horse in the race that you're doing a good job, and it was also nice to hear that a couple that wasn't in distress appreciated the metaphor of the pillars.

It was that day that I resolved to write this book so that this information could be shared with individuals and couples whom I didn't have the opportunity to work with in counseling. (And here's a special thanks to Buddy for serving as a four-legged nudge in that direction!)

**Empathy, mindfulness, humility, openness/presence, enthusiasm/curiosity, gratitude, honesty.**

What do they all have in common? They all help hold up your marriage, giving it the strength it needs to survive life's inevitable tremors and lurches without buckling.

If knowledge is power, you now have the power to start shaping your marriage. Having these pillars in mind as you go about your day takes no time at all, but earnestly holding that awareness is the first step in noticing things about your relationship—and yourself—that you might not have noticed before. You will likely recognize pillars that you've already built (without even labeling them as such or previously being aware of the words to describe those already-strong traits and habits). You will probably identify areas that are shakier and need shoring up. You will start to see how, like you and your partner, the pillars work in concert, how characteristics overlap at times, how one relies on the other(s).

Thank you for spending time with my thoughts, words, and ideas in the interest of strengthening such a vital part of your life—your marriage or long-term relationship. It has been my honor to be with you on this journey!

# 10. ABOUT THE AUTHOR

Rich Nicastro, Ph.D., is a psychologist and couples counselor. With over two decades of experience, he has worked with hundreds of individuals and couples on a wide range of relationship and intimacy issues.

In addition to running his private practice, Dr. Nicastro has lectured at several universities and conducts workshops on a variety of marital and relationship topics. His relationship advice has appeared on television, radio, and in national magazines.

He is passionate about helping couples create deep emotional connections and believes that healthy relationships give meaning and fulfillment to our lives. His goal is to guide individuals and couples as they implement the skills that will allow their marriage/relationship to flourish. He and his wife make their home in New Mexico.

Dr. Nicastro can be reached at www.StrengthenYourRelationship.com or www.HowToSpiceUpYourMarriage.net.

Manufactured by Amazon.ca
Bolton, ON

21040431R00096